MY RURAL COMMUNITY

Portia Summers

Enslow Publishing
101 W. 23rd Street
Suite 240
New York, NY 10011
USA
enslow.com

WORDS TO KNOW

community—A group of people who live and work together.

crops—Plants grown to make food or other products.

hands—People on a farm who do most of their work with their hands.

harvest—Pick crops, or the time of year when crops are picked.

rural—In the country.

service—An act that is helpful.

surgery—An operation that a doctor does to treat a patient.

veterinarian—A doctor who treats animals instead of people.

CONTENTS

In a rural community there is a lot of land, and houses are far apart from each other.

Life in the Country

A community is a group of people who live and work together. There are many different kinds of communities. In a city community, a lot of people live close together. In a rural, or country, community, people are spread out over a large area. There are not many buildings. People in the country work together to help each other in many ways.

Children in the Country

Children who live in the country may not have neighbors with other children close by. At home, they usually help with chores around the house and then play with their brothers and sisters. They may explore the fields or streams around their house. After school, they may take part in after-school programs. These programs might include sports teams or clubs. They learn about what it means to be a part of their community.

Getting to School

Because there aren't many kids around, most kids have to take a long ride on the school bus to go to class. Kids from more than one town may share a single school.

Most children who live in a rural community take a bus to school.

Growing Up on a Farm

Many of the people who live in rural communities live on farms. They grow food for themselves and for everyone else to eat. Lots of young people join clubs to learn how to be farmers when they grow up. They learn how to work with animals. They learn how to grow plants. They learn how to use the kinds of machines they need to use to run a farm. These clubs are run by members of the community. They make sure that young people in the rural community will have the tools they need to succeed.

A girl holds her prize-winning chicken.

What Does a Farmer Do?

It takes a lot of work to run a farm. Farms may be small or large. On a small farm, the farmer and his family might do most of the work themselves. On a big farm, the farmer will pay for extra help called farm hands. They might be hired to drive tractors and trucks. Hands might help the farmer fix machinery. Other farm hands might help to pick the crops.

Being a farm hand is hard work. Sometimes these people work on a farm all year long. Other times they only work for a few weeks, when there is extra work to do. These workers make up a part of the rural community.

Workers on the Go

All over the country, different crops are ready to be picked at different times of the year. Some workers travel from place to place, working on a different farm every week.

Field hands weed a crop of spinach.

Caring for Animals

The veterinarian, or vet, is part of the rural community too. A vet is a doctor for animals. The vet visits the farm to take care of the animals. She tries to keep the animals from getting sick. She helps animals that are hurt or sick get better. She may give them medicine or do surgery, just like doctors do for humans. A vet in the rural area also takes care of the pets that are part of the community. Pet owners bring their pets to the vet's office for care.

A calf gets a checkup from the vet.

Kinds of Farms

There are many different kinds of farms. Each farmer has a special job. Some farmers raise animals. Others grow crops, such as wheat or apples. Let's learn about some of these farms.

What Happens on a Wheat Farm?

A wheat farmer grows wheat. The wheat gets turned into flour to make bread, noodles, and cake. To make all that food, the farmer has to take care of the wheat plants from the time they are seeds until they are ready to harvest. He has to make sure the wheat has plenty of water and plenty of sun. These crops are sold to other people in the community. They are also sold in large communities that cannot grow their own wheat.

A harvester is a large machine that helps farmers gather crops. It is much faster and easier than harvesting by hand.

How Does a Dairy Farm Work?

Dairy farms are a special kind of farm found in the rural community. On a dairy farm, the farmer raises cows for milk. Twice a day, the farmer brings the cows into the barn and milks the cows. A truck driver comes and picks up the milk from the farmer. The truck driver is part of the rural community. He or she takes the milk to a dairy. At the dairy, they make butter, cream, and milk for people in the community.

Who Milks the Cows?

On a small farm, people might be in charge of milking the cows. Sometimes the farmer's children have this job. But on a large farm with lots of cows, milking by hand takes too much time. On these farms, machines milk the cows! It is much faster, and as many as twenty cows can be milked at one time.

Neighbors in a Rural Community

Many people who live in the country like to go to town to meet with other members of the community. Since people in rural communities live far apart, visits to town allow them to talk with neighbors about what is happening in their lives. They might also go shopping or eat at a diner. Here they are able to share news with other people in the community. Often they share ideas and help each other with problems.

Going to the Fair

In the summertime, people from all over the countryside get together at the fair. There are contests to see who raises the best animals and who bakes the best pie. At the fair, people can go on rides and play games.

Getting Gas

People in a rural community sometimes need to drive a long way to meet with people or to buy things that they need. The person who owns the gas station is an important member of the rural community. He or she provides gas for cars, tractors, or other machines. Gas allows cars and machinery to run. The gas station owner gives the community an important service.

The gas station is an important part of the rural community.

Helping Each Other

People who live in the country count on one another for help. If you need to borrow a tool, your neighbor will share his with you. He may even help you do the work you need to do. He knows you will help him too. Even though the houses are far apart, people who live and work in a rural community are very close.

Neighbors in a rural community are happy to lend a helping hand when there is work to be done.

ACTIVITY: JOBS ON THE FARM

There are a lot of jobs that need to be done on a farm. Many people may be needed to grow crops and raise animals. Let's look closer at the farm community and the work that different people do there.

1. Make a list of some crops (vegetables, fruits, grains, etc.). Next, list some animals that might live on a farm.
2. From your lists, choose one crop or animal (apples, for example).
3. Do some research online to learn more about your crop or animal. How is it grown or raised? What kind of work is needed to make the crop grow? How are the animals taken care of?
4. Make your own graphic organizer like the one on page 23. In the center oval, write the name of your crop or animal. In each circle around it, list one of the jobs that people must do with that crop or animal. (See the examples given on page 23.)
5. Look at your organizer once it is complete. How many different jobs did you come up with? It takes a lot of work and a lot of people to make a farm run!

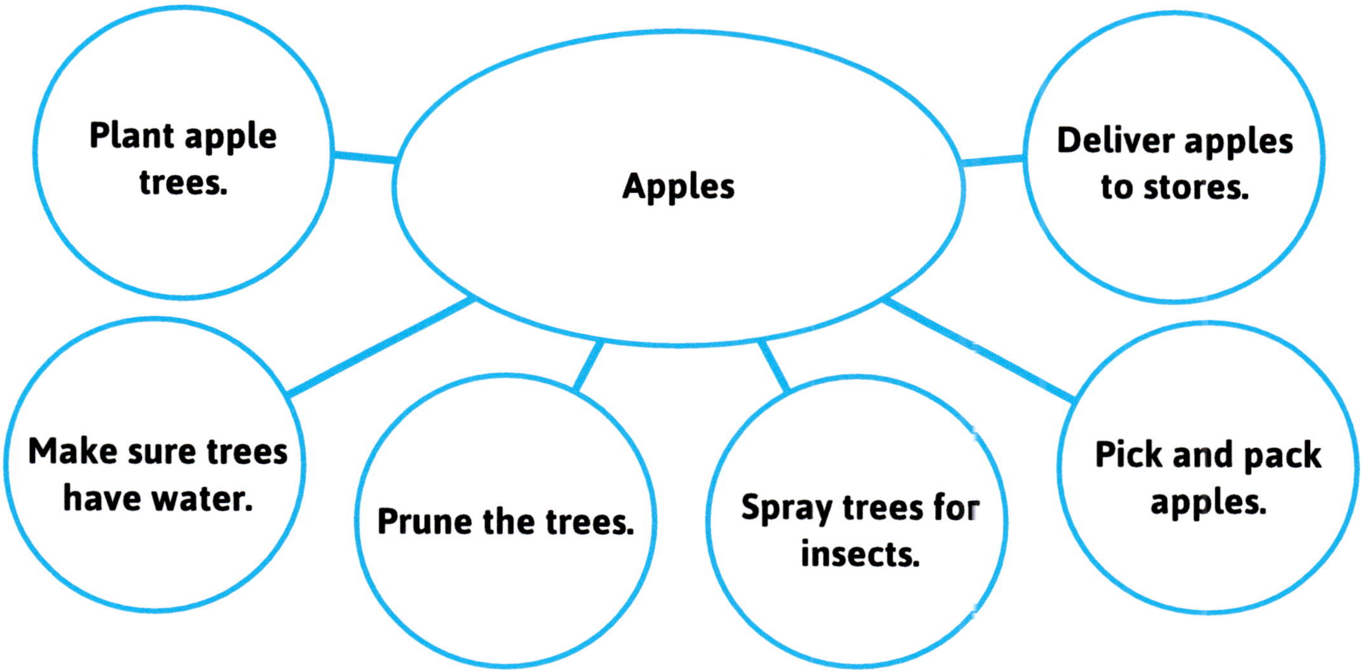
Apples
Plant apple trees.
Deliver apples to stores.
Make sure trees have water.
Prune the trees.
Spray trees for insects.
Pick and pack apples.

LEARN MORE

Books

Edwards, Clint. ***Show Me Community Helpers.*** Mankato, MN: Capstone, 2013.

Hunter, Rebecca. ***Farmer.*** Twickenham, UK: Tulip, 2014.

Keiser, Cody. ***We Live on a Farm.*** New York: PowerKids Press, 2016.

Royston, Angela. ***Diary of a Farmer.*** Chicago: Heinemann, 2014.

Websites

Dairy Farming Today

dairyfarmingtoday.org/Life-On-The-Farm/Pages/DayInTheLife.aspx

A day in the life of a dairy farmer.

My American Farm

myamericanfarm.org/classroom/games

Learn all about farms, soil, crops, and food.

INDEX

Published in 2017 by Enslow Publishing, LLC.
101 W. 23rd Street, Suite 240, New York, NY 10011

Library of Congress Cataloging-in-Publication Data
Names: Summers, Portia, author.
Title: My rural community / Portia Summers.
Description: New York : Enslow Publishing, 2017. | "2017 | Series: Zoom in on communities | Audience: K to Grade 3. | Includes bibliographical references and index.
Identifiers: LCCN 2015047561| ISBN 9780766078208 (library bound) | ISBN 9780766078154 (pbk.) | ISBN 9780766078185 (6-pack)
Subjects: LCSH: Farm life--Juvenile literature. | Neighbors--Juvenile literature. | Communities--Juvenile literature.
Classification: LCC HT421 .S86 2016 | DDC 307.72--dc23

LC record available at http://lccn.loc.gov/2015047561
Printed in Malaysia

To Our Readers: We have done our best to make sure all website addresses in this book were active and appropriate when we went to press. However, the author and the publisher have no control over and assume no liability for the material available on those websites or on any websites they may link to. Any comments or suggestions can be sent by e-mail to customerservice@enslow.com.

Photo Credits: Cover, pp. 1, 4 Joseph Sohm/Shutterstock.com; graphics throughout Kev Draws/Shutterstock.com (people circle), antoshkaforever/Shutterstock.com (people holding hands), 3d_kot/Shutterstock.com (houses); p. 7 Frank Whitney/Getty Images; p. 8 Erik Isakson/Getty Images; p. 11 Nancy Nehring/iStock; p. 12 135pixels/Shutterstock.com; p. 14 mihalec/Shutterstock.com; p. 16 WitthayaP/Shutterstock.com; p. 18 Kenneth Sponsler/Shutterstock.com; p. 19 © AP Images; p. 21 Elizabethsalleebauer/Getty Images.